# FAITH IN THE BROKEN PLACES

## GLORIA WIGGINS

## Contents

| | |
|---|---|
| THANKFUL | 4 |
| INTRODUCTION | 5 |
| DEDICATION | 6 |
| YOUNG ME | 7 |
| TEENAGE ME | 11 |
| A NEW BEGINING | 13 |
| QUESTIONS | 18 |
| A PAIN THAT HURTS TO THE BONE | 20 |
| MY HEART BROKEN INTO PIECES | 24 |
| WHY? WHEN? DID I DO SOMETHING WRONG? | 26 |
| DEATH A KNOCKING | 29 |
| BREAK THROUGH | 31 |
| THE WORD OF TRUTH | 34 |
| WHEN HE CALLS | 36 |
| PEACE THROUGH THE STORM | 37 |
| FEAR FROM THE PAST | 40 |
| GOD'S PROMISES ARE TRUE | 42 |
| MY MIRACLE | 45 |
| Prayer | 49 |

**Faith in the Broken Places**
*Gloria Wiggins*
Copyright © 2022. All Rights Reserved.

Published by:
Anointed Words Publishing Co.

All Rights Reserved. No part of this book may be used or reproduced in any manner whatsoever without the expressed written permission of the author. Address all inquiries to:

Email: awpubco@gmail.com

ISBN:

Printed in the United States of America

# THANKFUL

My Lord and Savior Thank you for letting me know that this was time to start to write this book. For giving me the courage and strength to move forward knowing your hand is in all I do.

# INTRODUCTION

IN THIS BOOK I HAVE POURED ALL OF ME, AND I HOPE IT CAN HELP SOMEONE GET TO THEIR BREAKTHROUGH AND SHOW THEM THAT YOU CAN BE GOING THROUGH THE HARKEST OF DAYS BUT THERE IS LIGHT AT THE END OF THE TUNNEL.

AND GOD ALWAYS LISTENING AND WALKING HAND IN HAND WITH YOU

SOME PEOPLE ASK GOD WHERE WERE YOU WHEN I WAS GOING THROUGH THIS AND THAT. WHY DID'NT YOU DO SOMETHING ABOUT MY ABUSE, MY RAPE, MY BROKEN MARRIAGE, MY CHILDREN IN DRUG, MY LOVED ONE DYING, ME LOSING MY JOB, LOOSING IT ALL.

AND GOD SAYS I WAS THERE THROUGH IT ALL. IT COULD HAVE BEEN WORSE IF I WAS NOT. YOU ARE STANDINFG, YOU ARE LIVING BECAUSE THROUGH ALL THIS YOU HAVE BEEN THROUGH IT WAS ME WHO WAS PATCHING EVERY SCAR, AND CLEANING THE NASTY THINGS IN YOUR LIFE, WHEN YOU WERE GOING DOWN THAT DARK HOLE IN LIFE.

IT WAS ME THAT IN YOUR LONELY NIGHTS WHERE YOU THOUGHT NO ONE COULD SEE YOU CRY AND POUR OUT YOUR SOUL ON THAT BEDROOM FLOOR. I SENT ANGELS TO PICK UP EVERY TEAR AND CLOTHED YOU WITH MY MERCY.

I WAS THERE WHEN NO ONE BELIEVED IN YOUR HOPES AND DREAMS AND YOU'RE STANDING STRONG BECAUSE I WAS THERE. I'M YOUR GOD AND WILL NEVER FORSAKE YOU.

# DEDICATION

This book is dedicated to my husband Craig and our son Kraig because of them I wouldn't be sitting here writing this book. I am so thankful each day for my little family. I am truly blessed.

To all who have prayed and gave me words of encouragement thank you. I want to say a special thank you to my Pastors Michael and Kim Lyons here in Lima who always have been there when we needed a word or just an ear to listen and prayer. To my Pastors Ramon and Miriam Matos back home in Michigan I also thank you for your prayers and love and also the word when we needed to hear it.

Yorden, KJ, Kraig and our other angel babies who we never got to meet. I am a mom because of you.

**_Like my Pastor always says: HERE WE GO!!!!_**

# YOUNG ME

I was born and raised in Pontiac, Michigan. We lived in the projects and just grew up in where people might say the rough neighborhood. We saw a lot of things, but these things do not make you the person you are.

When I was a little girl, I loved playing mom and playing with dolls and just being really girlie I played pretend with my siblings, and I always played the mom roll. Just a girly girl.

At the age of 5 years old I remember how a close friend of the family telling me to come sit on his lap, and how he took advantage of the way I was with everyone that came into my life as far as trusting them and loving them and also respecting my adults when they said something to me.

(As many of you have probably been in these shoes where you have been taken advantage of molested, raped etc. Know that these people are sick

and they need help and that it is not your fault someone hurt you. Let God come into your life and heal you from all you been through, and know you are not alone.)

I thought what was happening to me and what he was doing to me was normal because he would say no one needs to know and that I was his special friend. I learned to stay quiet, and this lasted a couple of years.

Now a second person came into the picture and was having his way with this little girl who was scared to speak on what was happening to her.

These men would say I was special to them and that what they were doing was because they loved me and that it was just a

# FAITH IN THE BROKEN PLACES

game we were playing. I was 8 years old when it all stopped, I guess I was getting older and sooner or later I was going to talk.

And this age mom had started the talk with me and well even then I did not speak on what had happen to me. I was scared that I would get in trouble, and no one would believe me.

By the age of 10 years old I felt more like a grown up and not another kid. I had feelings that no little girl should ever feel.

I never said anything to anyone. After getting a little older I knew better and that what these men did to me was wrong and sick. That they took advantage of my innocence. I would see them once in a while I never said anything to anyone and well this book only speaks of my experiences and not exposing anyone. I know and have seen what Gods hands can do when someone does one of his little ones wrong. He is a just God.

Think back I felt like I grew up to fast. I was not fast as some would call it. I never did anything to show what had happen to me years prior.

No one knew or knows all I went through till now that I am writing this book.

I do not blame anybody for what I went through. These two men who did these things have paid for their sins.

Like I said before I felt like I grew up to fast. I liked hanging around the older kids and the adults. Everyone I hung out with were always older than me. I felt like I was an adult just like them. That I was just grown so I thought.

By me being this way, I saw a lot of things deceit, cheating, betrayal some people were just not loyal. I saw people go through pain and disappointment and seeing some these people around me deal with their heartaches was like wow. I would say I don't want to cry like they did or be like they were. I don't want to be the one causing anyone any pain or breaking anyone's heart. I wanted that when I was their age that I was different.

At times I thought that maybe that's how life was. That everyone who was an adult had to live this way. I heard a lot of! DON'T TRUST NO ONE! Some people just like hurting others and they are not for you.

By 12 years old I was very guarded and just did not think like a kid no more I was in Junior High School and had my friends and just acted older. I didn't think like a kid or did kid things did like play outside and things like that. I was mentality different.

I liked boys and at that age I got my first boyfriend we went to the same school for a little bit because he was 2 grades ahead of me. (I can say I am married to him now lol) As you read along you will hear more about us and our journey.

We were together for 2 1/2 years we skipped school we were together all the time. We got ourselves into a lot of trouble just because we wanted to be together all the time.

After 2 1/2 years of being together we had step over what my parents would say you trying to grow up to fast you're not ready for real life. We crossed some boundaries and just was moving too fast.

So, we were told we could not see each other any longer or be around each other anymore and that if we were meant to be then destiny would bring us back together one day. This decision changed me and filled me with so many emotions and just why was the one person I trusted and loved was taken away from me.

# FAITH IN THE BROKEN PLACES

I rebelled and I was very angry. For a long time, I had thought I had lost my best friend, and I would never see him again. This was not fair at all.

I hurt people along the way including my parents who I apologize to till this day for being hard headed and just not being the best daughter and for being that way. Even to my siblings I was not a good big sister to them.

I thought life was over for me thinking of course like a teenager. Now that I have a child of my own, I understand so much what my parents really wanted was for me not to walk in their footsteps. And why they had rules.

Every time my parents said anything to me it was like they were the enemy I wanted to be grown so fast, and I just did not care about how I was making my mom feel. Now that am older, I wish I would have

listened to my parents more especially mom because I know I put her through some heart ache and how many tears she cried for me being so hard headed for that I am sorry always.

Her rules were not to hurt me she always wanted the best for her kids and if that meant tough love then she did what she had to. I am glad she was the way she was with me. And even though I failed her so many times as a daughter I am happy we have the greatest relationship now.

Life is too short, and your mom could be here today and gone tomorrow you may not like all the things parent has to say even being and adult, but honor them one day you will have children of your own and you will understand all the sleepless nights and tears and prayers that your parents did for you.

# TEENAGE ME

I needed to get out of my house. I am tired of the rules and found myself at the age of 15 and 16 years old all attitude out. I smoked weed and drank and loved the party scene. I did not care about anything.

At the age of 16 years old I met another guy. We hit it off right away. He was my second serious boyfriend. Things got a little carried away between us, and well I got engaged at 17 years old. Planning a wedding and yes again moving fast without a care in the world.

I was going to get married. I remember my mom asking if I was sure about what I wanted to do I said yes. I was going to get married and that was that.

Getting married I would leave my parents' house. I would be doing things right in their eyes and just make them proud of me. And I wouldn't have to follow their rules.

At the age of 17 years old getting ready for a change I was not even ready for.

(If you're a teenager reading this book. Enjoy being a teenager and having fun and graduations and planning for college and your future. Let God be your guide when we make decisions without him our plans do not work.)

I did not graduate with my friends or get ready for college. Instead, I was sitting on my bedroom floor planning a wedding.

I got married 4 months after turning 18 years old. I did not know how to be a wife. I did not know how to even cook much. Here I was married to someone who showed his true colors on our wedding and well I was stuck with him because divorce was not

## FAITH IN THE BROKEN PLACES

an option. He had his own issues and insecurities, and he was not happy in the choices he had made for his own life.

We had good times and bad times. I will not be going into detail about this period in my life it was just not a good time always.

But I can say there were years where I thought I should just run and go and then there were times I just stayed because that was the right thing and Godly thing to do. I won't say things ended on a good note because it did not. I was broken, hurt and only by God's grace I am alive.

6 Years is a long time to live like you don't know what the next year would bring or hear that their life was miserable because of you. Or if you ever will see another 6 years.

We had no children together and after 6 years we had moved on and I filled for divorce, and I had given my life to Christ and was living for him and him alone. God was speaking to my life and restoring what man had destroyed.

Change was coming, love was coming, and I was receiving every word he was giving me through his prophets and to my spirit.

I was broken for such a long time that I would have rather be alone and not go through the heart ache I went through.

I was by myself for 3 years and was learning to love me and serve God and keep me on the right path.

(Prayer is the key to overcome all pain and suffering. It is the only thing that helped me not lose my mind and make through the trials I went through. Pray without seizing God is listening)

# A NEW BEGINING

PROVERBS 31: 10-12

Who can find a virtuous wife? For her worth is far above rubies. The heart of her husband safely trusts her; So, he will have no lack of gain. She does him good and not evil all the days of her life.

I remember December 2004 we had just lost one of my uncles and this was such a hard blow for our family. I was in charge of the funeral, and it was just something that really hurt my family.

I remember sitting in my stepdad's apartment on his computer just searching for different things and I typed my first boyfriends name and boom I had all his information including a picture and this had put something in my heart to do so I did just that.

Who says the internet is evil it is not all bad. It is not evil when you are using it for the right information and not something that is not good for your soul.

I sat in front of that computer what seemed for hours, but I knew what I needed to do.

After all this happen, I sat in my room and was speaking to God and I told him that before the year ends, I will apologize to all the people who I have hurt or even thought I hurt. I want 2005 to be a fresh start without any baggage. So many people were on that list, and I did, in some way, wanted to apologize to each of them.

He was on my list, and I wrote him the letter, sent him that letter December 13. I explained to him what I was doing and the reason for the letter, and that all I wanted was his forgiveness for all the things I got us into when we were younger, I told him

## FAITH IN THE BROKEN PLACES

a little about what happen after we were separated from my parents.

Thinking: Wow after all this time 12 years later I had found my first boyfriend. And I am able to tell him what I felt about losing him. I was happy that I was going to have closer from that time in my life. So, I thought this was closer and not the beginning of something.

When your heart is torn to pieces, and you don't really see how broken you have been. You lose faith and hope in everything the only one you can trust is God, he has never failed you.

God had changed my life and was working all aspects of my life.

(God knows you he can change your life in an instant if he wants to. We just have to trust in him)

Going back a little to when I was 15 years old my mom had taken me to my OB appointment. It was the first time I am finding out that I was not going to be a mom. I had PCOS (polycystic ovarian syndrome), and the Dr looked at me and said bluntly you will never conceive and have children. At that moment I did not make a big deal about it, but as I got older my feelings changed. I wanted to be a mom. But when God has plans for your life, no Dr can change his plans.

I had so many issues I was dealing with. I did not feel pretty or liked I did not feel important. I never thought I was going to be happy. This was life, right? WRONG!! I was destroyed from my past that I could not see anything else. God was doing something behind the scenes things I did not know or even would have thought of he was making a new me.

A woman who was going to find love and have new blessings in her life.

A year after finding my first boyfriend he had sent me a letter back and that was the start of something. 362 letters and lots of phone calls.

We got engaged and I was planning a wedding. But this time around it was different I was an adult, and God was in the mist of it all. I had people bless us with everything we needed for our wedding the only thing I paid for was my dressed. God was touching people and sending them our way to bless our wedding. When things are from God. He supplies all your needs. We were beyond blessed.

Two months before getting married God spoke to my life giving me a prophetic word using the Pastors wife and he said that he was going to bless me with a child, and that he will be like Samuel. I received that word in my heart, and I believed it. My faith was activated.

We got married March 4, 2006, and it was like a dream come true and this time God was in it all. Six months after getting married we had received the news that I was pregnant excited and just happy to know that the Dr that told me years ago was wrong on his diagnoses and lie. That happiness did not last long a month after finding out that I pregnant we had a miscarriage.

I could yet again hear that Dr in my head at the age of 15 telling me I was never going to be a mother. As a couple we cried together, and it was a cry we had thought at the time we had never cried before. Confused and destroyed we moved forward and just kept the faith that one day it will happen for us.

After being in our hometown for what seemed all our lives. Two years after getting married we decided to move. We moved to Ohio, before moving we had suffered another miscarriage. It is like your heart breaks every time you hear people ask why? when? Are you doing something wrong? It is devastating.

# FAITH IN THE BROKEN PLACES

Your broken you don't understand why things like this are happening to you or if you were doing something wrong.

Moving to Ohio was the best decision we made. The right thing to do. We started fresh and we loved the area we had moved into.

We have been here going on 14 years.

(I don't know who I can help by telling you about me. Sometimes God has to move you from your comfort place and send you to the unfamiliar, he unknown. So that he can give the things he wants and has for life. The best things are given by him when you are in your uncomfortable places. He has a lot for us we just have to let him take over sometimes)

I feel like our move made us better people. And even though some people think we moved to get away from them or because we thought we were better than them or that we don't need anybody else. This is all far from the truth. Because of us making this decision my husband found the welding job he was looking for; we bought our first home and even though family is not here we did this for us.

We moved here for change for healing to have a better future and to also start our family. The one that God had promised us. Trust me it was not an easy move for us, but we knew it had to happen.

We got pregnant 2 years after are move and yet again we were dealing with another heart ache. I had a tubal pregnancy. Dr said we can remove the tube, or we can give you a shot. Surgery was cutting my chances of conceiving and make that percentage low. The shot would save the fallopian tube, and you would have to grow through some pain till the pregnancy is dissolved and a miscarriage would happen. No option helped my pain. I wanted to become a mother, and it was taken from me again.

I remember calling my husband who was working in Chicago at the time and asking him what should I do? I was scared I was confused and alone I wanted us to make the decision together. He was 4 hours away we had no family here this was a new thing for me.

We decided on the shot. It was a week before we had the miscarriage it was a painful process not only physically but mentally. Broken and lost I felt like somethings was really wrong with me.

Discouraged, tired and just simply torn inside and even then, we kept moving forward. One thing I can say at this point in our lives we had stop seeking God and we just dealt with our pain in our own way. Without the comforter to comfort us the pain sometimes feels unbearable.

The hardest thing to do. Is to deal with lost and pain without God in the midst of your storms he is the only one who could help us when we go to him it makes the healing process would come faster if we did that.

GALATIANS 6:9

Let us not grow weary doing good for in due season we shall reap if we do not lose heart.

# QUESTIONS

We dealt with the why? when? Did you do something wrong? Questions once again more on my end then anything because I guess I'm the woman and I suppose to be reproducing. Well, I remember saying if I needed to stand on my head for it I probably would, but it does not work that way.

(Don't listen to these who don't believe in your hopes and dreams, and don't believe that God said he was going to do it. To these who don't believe God's promise for you just tell them to sit back and just watch)

Words a woman who has the heart of a mother does not need to hear. You still have no kids? When you think it's going to happen? You aren't getting any younger. Come on people be nice.

PLEASE! PLEASE! stop these comments. The hurt that these people make you feel is not good. Takes you to another level makes you feel like less than a woman, like God forgot about you. Maybe I'm not good enough maybe I won't be a good mom. Maybe that's why I am losing my baby's.

Still longing for a child, it was looking so far away.

I remember my husband saying this for my future, everything we are doing and have is for our son or daughter.

Man, we're not getting any younger. These were the desires of his heart. I started praying and asking God to please give us a child not for me but for my husband so that he could believe and know who God truly is and that He does miracles.

Our marriage got hits left and right because of us not having children and I think people just made it worst by their comments opinions and not having faith this couple was ever going to be parents one day.

PROVERBS: 22:29

Do you see a man who excels in his work? He will stand before kings; he will not stand before unknown men

## A PAIN THAT HURTS TO THE BONE

My husband still working on the road and coming home on weekends or every other week or sometimes even a month at the time, depending on where work was hard.

The reality was that this was tough at times. But he did this mostly to stay busy, for us to have the things we had and to keep building for our future which was kids.

In 2016 we had renewed our vows for our 10-year anniversary, and it was a beautiful ceremony. And even on this day God used my Pastor from Michigan who came to do the ceremony for us and he gave us a word in front of like 40 to 50 people and he said that God had brought us together and he was going to bless us. We found out a month later we were having a baby again.

It was my first longest pregnancy. This was baby #6 for us and just happy that everything was going smoothly. We did not know what we were having because every time we had an ultrasound done the baby would close its legs. But we did not care just as long as baby was healthy, we were ok with whatever Girl or Boy.

The rough part for me was the unknown after having 5 losses prior it was all just scary to me.

I remember that in June my husband had lost a close coworker and friend, he was more like a brother to him. They had room together for about 4 to 5 years while they worked on the road. That lost shook him to the core and till this day he will never forget that loss.

July was here and I had made to 20 weeks of that pregnancy.

On July 15, 2016, to be exact, I was at work. I was feeling a little crampy but nothing that worried me. I was standing there after helping a customer and I feel a little trickle. I went to the bathroom, and I saw a little mucus when I wiped.

I was not sure if this was my water breaking or what first time again going through this and even making it to 20 weeks of pregnancy. I felt like all of a sudden, my world stood still that day.

So, I told my boss I need to get to the hospital, and I drove there. On my way there I called my husband I told him what was going on.

We went from one hospital to another hospital that was 2 1/2 hours away. Contractions were starting to come like every 7 to 8 minutes but to me they were lasting an eternity because of my fears. Scared yet again with the feeling of hopeless and just what is going to happen.

I was feeling all sorts of emotions at the moment. There was no stopping this baby from coming.

When we get to the other hospital, we were told that it could be hours to a day before baby comes, they could not do anything because of the weeks that I was.

We were told so many things that the baby was not going to look normal that it might not be developed all the way. Be prepared for the worst is what it felt like. The worst was knowing that the baby was not going to make it. That once again we were going to have to deal with heart ache. I was completely devastated and lost.

PSALM 34:4

I sought the Lord, and he heard me and delivered me from all my fears.

# FAITH IN THE BROKEN PLACES

I prayed for my baby and asked God for his will to be done. I can see my husband falling apart and just trying to be there to comfort me was hard for him because he was already grieving from his friend passing away a month prior. He needed comforting himself. He had so many emotions going on that I did not know what I was going to get from him, he was angry, sad at having to go through this over and over again.

I can see his pain and how this was all breaking him and destroying the last bit if hope he had. This hurt me to the point I can feel the pain in my bones.

It was July 16th around 3 or 4 on the morning when my water had broken completely. The nurses rushed to the room, and they called my Dr as the rushed to get me ready for delivery. I remember the Dr looking at me and she said 2 or 3 pushes and baby will be out.

Like said before we did not know what we were having. We were going to meet him or her for the first time.

The unknown and not knowing what was going to happen or what we were going to see when the baby was delivered. This was so scary for the both of us and my mom who was with us through the whole thing. I did not open my eyes until they said that it was a girl and that she looked normal. I am not going to lie I was scared of the unknown.

Yorden Victoria was born at 14 ounces and 16inches long she was beautiful she was alive for 3 hours. We held her and kissed her, and we told her how much we loved her, and how much of a fighter she was. She looked like a normal baby no abnormalities she was all daddy from head to toes.

And till this day she is one of the reasons I fight the way I do for everything I set my mind to do and goals.

I fight because these three hours were the hardest three hours I had to go through. I fight for what I believe in and for everything I love and want in my life.

Because she fought till her last breath so shouldn't I who have lived here longer.

Isaiah 41;10

Fear not for I am with you be not dismayed for I am your God I will strength you, yes, I will help you, I will uphold you with my righteous right hand.

## MY HEART BROKEN INTO PIECES

Broken my heart torn into pieces, we buried our baby girl, and I tell you when people say a part of them went with their loved one when they passed away. I felt like it was true. But I tell you that the out pouring we had was amazing she was loved. So many people showed up to her funeral and the love and support that people showed was wonderful.

But when everyone was gone and the silence of the night came, it was just too quiet and still enough to hear my heart beat from my chest.

Tears, anger, and pain and all the loss just filled our home nothing made us fill better.

Our marriage was being tested from all angles. A lot of people who called themselves friends and were with us, used our pain against us. They even put us against each other. Our pain was their gain.

Again, the questions Why? When? Did you do something wrong re appeared. I could not believe that I was hearing these dumb questions once again. It was like I was being mocked and tortured.

I did not feel woman enough I did not feel worthy to even be alive. I felt defeated, beat down and just like even the world itself hated me. My world had been torn upside down.

We changed. My husband and I were just not in a good place. Our home had turned into a place of grief and blame.

My husband would say to me I cannot look at you. Cause every time I look at you, I see her my baby girl and it hurts.

At that time, I wish it would have been me who was gone and not her. I cried myself to sleep for a long time and even would sneak to her grave almost every day just to see if it was real. If I was still living the nightmare or was just a dream it was not, she was gone, and I had to deal with my grief.

But again, there is no mistakes with God. When he has a plan for your life, he will make you go through the fire the storm to get what he has in store for you.

I felt like I was Job, and my husband was his wife telling me to curse my God and die.

# WHY? WHEN? DID I DO SOMETHING WRONG?

Early February of 2017 we had found we were pregnant, yet again, 8 months after our baby girl's birth.

We were not in a good place, and I remember just feeling alone through it all. I was 2 months along and after a really bad situation happened in Early March that shook me and broke me to the core, we ended up with yet another miscarriage. That was baby #7 my faith in everything I'm not going to lie was crushed. This time it was not my body doing it but stress and heart break.

Let me tell you, at the time this all happen I had to take 3 pregnancy test, and this was not including the blood work or going to the health dept and getting tested there. Someone had told my husband that with us being in a bad place that I was probably telling him I was pregnant to keep him in our marriage.

He was in a bad place I was his enemy I was having the losses, and he was angry. I felt just like I should not even be alive. Until we receive the call that I needed to come in because I started bleeding horribly, he then believed me that yes there was a pregnancy there.

And then I was giving myself the questions that many had asked me before when I had my losses.

WHY?

Why do I keep going to through this am I really supposed to have children? WHEN?

When is this going to happen for me? If God said it was going to happen for me.

Did I do something wrong?

Did I do something wrong, who did I hurt, what have done so bad that I'm paying for it by losing my baby's?

But this was the enemy putting these questions in my mind. Why?

Because this was a process, I had to go through to make me grow and to help others that are in my shoes.

When?

In Gods time. His timing is perfect and when you get to the end of this book you will see why his timing is perfect.

Did I do something wrong?

The answer was No the process just needs to happen so that God can be glorified so his will be done in you.

We thought our marriage was over that we done with it all. We thought there was no hope for us.

We went through so many emotions the ups and downs and our lives were in a dark place. We were not seeking for Gods guidance and more on my husband end he just done.

We had lost a lot of friendship along the way. But it all had to happen so that we could heal and make it through all this together even though we were so far apart. God had some plans in store for us we just didn't know yet.

# FAITH IN THE BROKEN PLACES

PSALM 23:4

Yea, though I walk through the valley of the shadow of death. I will fear no evil; For you are with me; Your rod and your staff, they comfort me

# DEATH A KNOCKING

Death was calling, knocking and the devil was ready for our lives.

He took advantage of every emotion, every bad thought, pain everything we were going through and every time even a friendly gesture would happen between us it would turn into something negative.

I remember sitting in my Livingroom contemplating suicide and what I could do to just stop the pain. I hated life, I hated people, I hated myself this just had to be the way out from everything.

I felt like my losses were all my fault. I just wanted all the hurt I had to just go away.

But I remember God sending me a local Pastor my way she had come to my window one day when I was working, and we exchanged numbers. Till this day we are good friends, and I was able to talk to her about all I had been through knowing it was going to stay confidential. She listened and prayed over me. But still, I did not give my life in full to the Lord.

I remember also listening to a song called Thy will be done, and it spoke to my life. When you do not understand his will and what he wants for your life. We just got to know that he will be done in our lives he does have the last word, and he is with you through whatever heart ache you are going through.

Thinking of my husband, having to go through another burial, his babies gone and now his wife. I did not want to do this to him. Another loss was not an option. My family would have been devastated and of course I knew if I went through with it, I wouldn't see my babies again.

## FAITH IN THE BROKEN PLACES

If you ever going through a process of hurt loss, pain that unbearable. Remember death is not going to resolve the issue it will add pain to these you left behind who love you and need you in some shape or form in their lives.

To relieve some of what I was feeling. I started cutting and taking pills to help me just sleep. Depression had overwhelmed me and taken over my life at this point felt numb at times spaced out at times. And to the blind eye I was fine living life and being just plain old me.

I remember my husband just telling me over again. How he had given up on all he wanted in life. He wanted to be done with it all. He wanted done with life and done with this marriage. He was dealing with his own demons and emotions, feelings, pain, anger he was broken himself.

When a man can't fix it, the easy way out is to walk away.

And all I wanted was for things to be ok, and for something to just help us get through what we were going through.

BUT GOD! BUT GOD! BUT GOD!

He always comes on time.

PSALM 107 19:20

Then they cried out to the Lord in their trouble. And he saved the out of their destresses.

He sent his word and healed them and delivered them from their destructions.

# BREAKTHROUGH

In 2017 I think God was like it is time for me to show this couple who I really am. And that when I say I am going to do something I do it in my time and my will is always done.

I remember we had decided one day to go get dinner and get some movies.

On our way to the video store my husband started talking to me about how I could keep the house, and he would make sure I was taken care of. He would make sure I didn't need anything.

He wanted a divorce he just could not do this anymore he said his pain and all we have been through years prior were just too much for him to bare.

We got to the video store and the conversation ended with me just telling him that it was not what I wanted and that I was willing to fight for us and our marriage.

We went into the store, got our movies, and we got in line. As we were standing there we were behind a man (who we now call our Pastor and spiritual father.)

Who knew huh???

He turned around and looked at us with a smile on his face and he looked at my husband and said Wow! You look like my nephew but you probably ain't a knuckle head like he is. We all laughed. He told us to have a good day and that was that. So, we thought.

We paid for our movies and as we were walking out that man, we were just talking to was standing between the doors. With a smile on his face, he stopped us, and He speaks.

# FAITH IN THE BROKEN PLACES

I promise I am not stalking you guys, it's just that something is drawing me to you. Especially you and he pointed to my husband.

Wont God do it. He will point you out when he knows there is a need. When the situation is URGENT!!!

He began to say let me cut to the chase I am a Pastor we looked at each other.

This is when the shift happened. When God was like yeah, I sent you someone. It is time for breakthrough.

I remember we looked at each other as he was talking. With goosebumps when he said he was a Pastor because I knew in my spirit something was coming from this conversation.

He said I want you to be my special guest for Easter Sunday. Which was a week away. He handed my husband the card.

My husband says to him I'll be there. And in my heart and mind I'm like ok will see. Just because of the conversation we had in the car.

Plus, Easter being a week away a lot can happen in 7 days.

Things were still tough, and we went through that week just staying busy and just out of each other's way.

The card that Pastor gave us was on a magnet on the refrigerator door.

Saturday came and I remember it was late, and I was doing laundry and getting everything ready for the next week. I asked my husband the big question. I asked him if we were going to church on Sunday? Because you told the Pastor you will be there?

Not even looking at me still playing his game. He said, yeah get clothes ready, we are going.

God will move mountains he will do things in the unknown that we don't even see when he wants us for his kingdom.

Sunday morning was here, and my husband woke up early he had showered and was dressed and ready to go. I followed suit and got ready myself.

We were quiet on the way to church. We got there before service started. JEREMIAH 33:6

I will heal them and reveal to them the abundance of peace and truth

FAITH IN THE BROKEN PLACES

# THE WORD OF TRUTH

We made inside and sat down in the towards the middle isle. The church was packed.

I remember us sitting there and my husband said to me. It is loud in here and there is a lot of people. He said I feel sick to my stomach. He looked at me and said I'll be back I'm going to get some water.

I am sitting there thinking to myself. We going home we leaving. He doesn't want to be here.

He came back sat down. Still thinking to myself ok he quiet so asked him if he was ok and are we staying or leaving. He said we will stay I'll be alright.

All I can say is God you are amazing. This was the start of something great. PSALM 55:22

Cast your burden on the Lord, and He shall sustain you; He shall never permit the righteous to be moved.

God will resurrect the dead in you. He will make you see that he has been there all along.

The worship was great the songs all spoke to my heart especially the song Intentional. That really ministered to my soul.

As the Pastor came up and took the microphone, he didn't even know we were there sitting in the crowd.

God was already working in us. We had no idea the impact his message was going to have in our lives. God was going to do his thing.

The Pastor's message was powerful. I remember him speaking on loss and he spoke. You ask yourself why you had to bury your child and why such a loss? You ready to run and just leave it all and just ready to quit. Divorce is not an option, and my husband leans over and looks at me.

And he asked when did you talk to him. And I'm like I didn't talk to him. The only time we spoke to him was when we saw him at the video store.

As my eyes filled with tears. He sat there like he couldn't believe that this Pastor was preaching on all we have been through and just hitting every aspect of our lives.

God was pulling on heart strings and just letting us know he saw it all he was there the whole time.

When God is calling you, he will use a mule to speak to you if he has to. He will reach you no matter what. You can't keep running from his presence. Let God do he will heal you he will deliver you he will not forsake you. He knows you are broken and all you have been through just let him in your life and you will see.

FAITH IN THE BROKEN PLACES

# WHEN HE CALLS

PSALM 7:20-21

You, who have shown me great and severe troubles, shall revive me again, and bring me up from the depths of the earth.

You shall increase my greatness, and comfort me on every side.

Pastors' words were all God sent. These were for our lives. What we need to hear. Pastor did alter call, and he pressed on and spoke. I know there are people here who are ready to go be with their families and go eat there Easter dinners and just got celebrate.

But I am not leaving until the people God has spoken to come up. God is calling someone, and it is urgent. I knew it was us. He said I know God is working in someone life. I just can't leave.

I remember tears filled my eyes once again. The tears would not stop running down my face. My heart was raising. I looked at my husband and he had tears in his eyes. He grabbed me by my hand and took us up down the aisle and towards the alter.

When Pastors looked at us, he tells his leaders to stand and tells them. This is the couple I told you to pray for.

God's timing is always perfect and when he calls you here is no going back.

We gave our lives to God this day and we have been in our current church ever since and let me tell you God did not stop there.

# PEACE THROUGH THE STORM

In 2017 God was working in our lives. The healing had really started. We were two different people, who were not perfect but had work through the pain and suffering that had us bound.

We got pregnant once again with baby #8 and we were on cloud nine. This pregnancy was different, and we made it passed the 20-week mark, we thought of our baby girl Yorden and were happy to know we had pushed passed the pain of losing her.

I had made to six months it was just a different feeling we were at a place where we were trusting God and believing in him together. This time around we just were not leaning on our own strength we had something more in our lives and we were trusting and leaning on him.

Our marriage was stronger than it had ever been. There was love, compassion and understanding from one another.

At six months and a week we ended up in the hospital. We were sent to a hospital two hours away from home. Contractions had started and Dr's told us baby is coming early. We knew at the time that this was going to be a boy. We had nick named him KJ short for Kraig Jr.

November 1, 2017, the doctor comes in and says he needed to do an amnio to make sure there was no infection and that way if I delivered the baby early everything would be ok.

We get it done, and I tell you, it was a painful test to get done. But we waited what seemed like forever. Not thinking about what will happen next.

# FAITH IN THE BROKEN PLACES

Dr comes in and says without looking at me. Unfortunately, there is an infection and as right now the baby only has it. He will not make it after birth.

If we keep him in mom for a long period of time. Mom will get the infection also and she will get really sick, and she might not make it. And I looked at him and said what do we do there has to be something else do you even believe in God I know where I stand.

He looked at my husband you have a couple of hours to make a decision. Baby life or both lives.

Broken and confused I knew where I stood, and I asked my husband to get a second opinion. Because I was not making this decision.

He called our Pastor and our OBGYN back home and after listening to both of them and getting the advice he needed and getting prayer from our Pastor. He was ready to make a decision.

He called for the Dr and said I choose her life as he pointed towards me with tears in his eyes. I told him OK. They got me prepped for an epidural because my husband did not want me to go through the pain of labor. If we knew that our baby was not coming home with us. He wanted for me to be pain free.

They started the epidural and Pitocin to induce me. During this my blood pressure had dropped and kept dropping to the point I was out of it for a little bit.

November 2nd middle of the night I was weak and tired and just not ready for my baby boy to come yet.

After what felt like hours, they broke my water and baby boy was on his way. I gave three big pushes, and he was here. He weighed to pounds 16in long he looked just like his sister

Yorden. And just like her, we talked to him and told him we loved him. We told him it was ok for him to join his sister. He lasted 2 hours alive. He passed away in my mom arms. We will all see each other one day.

The room was peaceful it was it just a different grief. Don't get me wrong it hurt but Gods peace was all over us.

Even with all the precautions I still got the infection my baby boy had. It was bad I was in ICU for 7 days. The Dr would come in my room and ask me how I was feeling, and I would say I feel fine. The Dr would say that their test was showing them different results that my blood was going septic.

After days of antibiotics, they still were saying it didn't look good, and that things were not going to good if my blood levels didn't change. It was like the getting ready for me to die. While be on that floor you will hear the code blue alarms go of left and right and see nurse running to the room it was happening at. It was a scary experience.

2ND CORINTHIANS 5:17

Therefore, if anyone is in Christ, he is a new creation; old new things have passed way; behold, all things have become new.

I felt good I did not feel sick at all. I knew God's protection was over me. I had lost another baby, and all I wanted was to get out so I can lay him to rest. I needed to be ok, and God gave us that and more.

FAITH IN THE BROKEN PLACES

# FEAR FROM THE PAST

Was the fear there (YES) I remember my husband sitting across from me, and he never left my bed side. He could see the worry look in my face, and he asked me why you look so worried? I answered with tears in my eyes, I said because I don't know what's going to happen next.

What's going to happen after all this, and he said what do you mean what's going to happen next.

I said will you leave this time? Will you go back to how things were before, and you want to give up on us. Will I have to hear how much you hate me because I lost your child.

I told him that I did not like the look of disappointment in his eyes. It hurt me so much to see that.

He stood up and grabbed my hands and spoke. I know I have said and done things in anger because of our losses especially when we lost Yorden. But this time is different we are ok.

He said look at me because I had my head down, I looked up and he said We Are Ok. We are not going back to the darkness, and pain. We move forward.

This is what God does when he comes into your life. And changes darkness into light. We prayed together we cried together. We made it through that storm shining like gold, and it was the first time I didn't hear Why? When? Did you something wrong? That to me was a Wow moment.

REVELATION 21;4

And God will wipe away every tear from their eyes; there should be no more death, nor sorrow; nor crying. There should be no pain, for the former things have passed away.

2018 was on its way and God was really going to show out.

FAITH IN THE BROKEN PLACES

# GOD'S PROMISES ARE TRUE

God started doing something new in our lives in 2018. We went on our first vacation in May. We went to Key West. Our first honey moon since we had been married. We had a blast I overcame my fear of the ocean. Our time together was just awesome we laughed we did things we had never done. I say this was defiantly something we needed as a couple.

The same month after coming back from vacation. I got an invite to go preach at my church back home in Michigan. It was a great experience.

Again, God spoke to my life using the Pastor there and he said that since I was faithful, he was going to bless me with my heart's desire. They anointed me and prayed over my womb, and I felt a fire inside me that was sent from heaven like God was doing surgery right there. He said the miracle is coming soon.

I came home a couple days later and the following week. They had the women's conference. God did so many things in me this night I finally gave to him what was hurting me which was the ability to forgive something that was done to in 2017, and I left there that night.

Sunday service came right after that conference, and I remember one of the sisters came up to me and says I'm sorry I looked at her and said it's ok I did not understand why she was apologizing till she says. I felt something when all the ladies were told to pray for one another at the conference. and I did not say anything to you out of fear.

She says God is getting to do something in you and it's coming soon confirmation to the word that was spoken the week prior. I told her I receive it, and I believe it.

PSALM 100:4

Enter into his gates with thanksgiving, And into His courts with praise. Be thankful to Him and bless His name.

End of July of 2018 we find out we were pregnant with baby #9. And I remember when I told my husband did not believe me when I told him he was like are you sure. We got the blood work to confirm the pregnancy. And I tell you what we were ready for this.

Church theme for the year was NO MORE!!! God kept speaking to our lives, and he was showing us his wonders and all he was going to do through the pregnancy.

I remember we had a service were the preacher brought a big vase full of oil. And it was a powerful message, and everyone stood in line to get anointed and get a word or just prayer and I tell you what it was amazing. So, when it was our turned to go up Pastor Mike had oil coming down his arm. He grabbed my husband hand and held it high, (THIS TO ME WAS A SIGN OF VICTORY), and they poured the oil on our heads. He looked at his wife Pastor Kim and said give them a word. The word that was given was a break through word. And she said the curse has been broken and it was God had broken everything that was stopping his will to be done.

Our faith was stronger than ever, we knew this was it. This pregnancy was going to be a good one and we were going to receive our blessing.

When God gives you faith in the broken places. No one can take that hope and the miracle that comes from it away.

# FAITH IN THE BROKEN PLACES

We are living proof of this. Everyone who know us know that this journey was a tough one. It was tough for us. But through it all God was showing his power.

# MY MIRACLE

PSALM 23:3

He restores my soul; He leads me in the paths of righteousness for His name's sake.

We made month through months and was like wow this is really happening we getting closer and closer.

At 7 months my baby boy was trying to come early. My husband was working in Chicago. I called him and told him I was having contractions and was heading to the hospital to make sure I was not in active labor.

I get to the hospital, and they put the monitors on me. I was having contractions, but they were far in between not close together like if I was in active labor.

As I was waiting for my husband to get to the hospital. A good friend of ours showed up to the room I was in. He says that my hubby had called him and told him I was at the hospital, and he knew he was on his way there. I'll sit with you till he gets here. As we waited, we talk about all God was doing and had done.

When my hubby got to the hospital and made it to the room, I was in. You can see that worried look in his face. But even with that he was in good spirits.

He calls for the nurse to come in and he asked her what was going on? He just wanted to know.

He was not screaming or frustrated or rude like he would have been when we dealt with something like this in the past.

And I tell you again this is what God does when he is in control, and you give your life completely to him. He keeps you calm

# FAITH IN THE BROKEN PLACES

when everything is looking bad. Everything in his hands. God made the change in our lives. And it was time for a new season in our lives.

So, the tells him yes, your wife is having contractions, but they are not close together. We are going to start her on some medication to stop them. And see what happens.

But if this baby were to come tonight, he will be ok. He will live.

It was like a WOW moment for us. So, my husband says so you're telling me if he is born tonight, I will be a dad, and she will be a mom. She looks at him and says yes.

Well, the contractions stopped with the medication they gave me, and we went and had our baby shower. Which was such a wonderful turn out. The love and support that people showed us was amazing we were truly blessed.

Our dreams were playing themselves out right in front of us. Were happy to share our journey with people and just let them know God still does miracles. We have finally accomplished something big.

8 weeks after weeks after our hospital visit, we got induce and even thought I had to have a c-section because baby did not want to come when he was supposed to. We became parents third labor experience. But this time it was different. Our miracle was coming home with us.

And even though the devil tried to take my life because he was not happy that we received this miracle. So, my lungs filled with fluid, and I ended up in ICU. I got to hold him for a couple minutes, but God said no devil it is their time you do not win leave my children alone.

Our son was born April 2, 2019, Kraig Kristopher Noah. 7 pounds 12 ounces 18 1/2 inches long. Strong and with the cry of a warrior and healthy as can be. He was here and he was ours.

God gave me faith in the broken places my miracle had finally come to pass. When I had thoughts that I would never be a mother God showed out, and said here you go I keep my promises and I am faithful to my word.

When I got the why? when? Did you something wrong questions? Everyone who did ask me these questions had to sit back and look at what God had done for us.

Mathew 17:20

So, Jesus said to them, Because of your unbelief, for assuredly, I say to you, if you have faith as a mustard seed, you will say to this mountain, move from here to there, and it will move; and nothing will be impossible for you.

I hope through this book your able to receive a word of hope. That my testimony touches lives, and you can believe that there is faith in the broken places.

Loss can be so many things; losing a child, a friend, a loved one, a spouse, a job, a home. Whatever your loss is. Believe there is always hope and our God will not abandon you. He will always be there by your side seeing you all the way.

Don't let the Why? When? Are you doing something wrong? Questions keep you from having the faith and from believing that God can heal, restore the broken places in your life he did for me and my husband.

Be encouraged don't give up. If God said it, he will do it. In his time which is always perfect.

## FAITH IN THE BROKEN PLACES

I am happy to say I have enjoyed every moment with our miracle boy. He is funny and the most loveable 3-year-old right now.

And every time I look at him, I have no doubt that God is a miracle worker, and he will let you go through the fire so he can bring you out shining like gold and a new person in him.

I got Faith through my broken places. Seek and you will find in time that prayer works and that he still does miracles, signs, and wonders.

# PRAYER

Lord,

I thank you for the opportunity that you have given me to write this book. I thank you for all you have done for me and my family. Thank you for this new season. I pray for everyone who sits down to read this book. I asked that you blessed them and show them you are a faithful God. Bless their families give them the strength to heal. Especially these who are dealing with loss. They are not alone you are with them like you were with me.

Again, I thank you I give you the Glory and the honor because only you deserve it.

AMEN!!

Made in the USA
Middletown, DE
01 March 2025